Contents

Introduction

If you live in Europe or North America, it is likely that you take your food and water for granted. In other parts of the world, however, there are millions of people who struggle every day to find enough food and water to survive. Solving this problem is an urgent priority, but it also presents some serious challenges. Water and food are not readily available everywhere, and even if they were, not everyone would have access to the amounts that are consumed in more economically developed countries (MEDCs). There are simply not enough resources for everyone to use them at that level.

In MEDCs, more than enough food is available for the population and in some countries people suffer from health problems caused by eating too much.

A Global Problem

Food and water are considered to be basic human rights, which means that everyone should have enough of both to survive. Despite this, an estimated 840 million people were suffering hunger in 2006 and up to 1.5 billion lived without enough water. These figures refer to having just enough to survive. If the amount of food and water consumed by someone living in France or the United States was used as a measure of how much people should have, then these numbers would be even higher. This raises an important question about how much food and water we actually need. Many people in MEDCs now suffer health problems because they eat too much. Waste is another big issue. Vast quantities of food and water are wasted every day – food and water that could be helping to meet the needs of others.

Changing Trends

Long ago, people tended to grow just enough food to feed themselves and their families, and to trade within their communities. As societies developed and people travelled further afield, trade in food expanded and diets changed. In MEDCs in particular there was a move towards more meat-based diets, rather than traditional, largely vegetarian ones. The amount of meat being eaten has increased by more than 500 per cent in the past 50 years, and there are now more chickens on Earth than there are humans to eat them!

In recent years, processed foods have also become popular in MEDCs. The problem with these changing trends in diets is that making processed and meat-based food involves a lot more water, energy and other resources than traditional or vegetarian diets.

Another change has come about because of improvements in transportation and food technology such as refrigeration, packaging and preservation. In wealthier nations it is possible to buy strawberries in the middle of winter, fresh tomatoes all year round, and exotic fruits that could never be grown in the countries that import them. The demand for such items in MEDCs can place a strain on resources in other parts of the world – resources that include the water needed for growing and processing food.

All these issues have made governments, organisations and individuals think carefully about how food and water resources are used and shared out around the world. Providing a growing global population with enough food and water to keep them healthy, without damaging the environment or using up more resources than necessary, is a big challenge. However, there are a number of ways of developing the food industry more sustainably to help make sure there is enough for all.

EXPERT VIEW

'Each calorie of meat takes far more water to produce than a calorie of grain, so one of the simplest ways to increase the ratio of food produced to water consumed is to reduce dependence upon meat.'
COMPASSION IN WORLD FARMING, *REDUCING MEAT CONSUMPTION: THE CASE FOR URGENT REFORM*

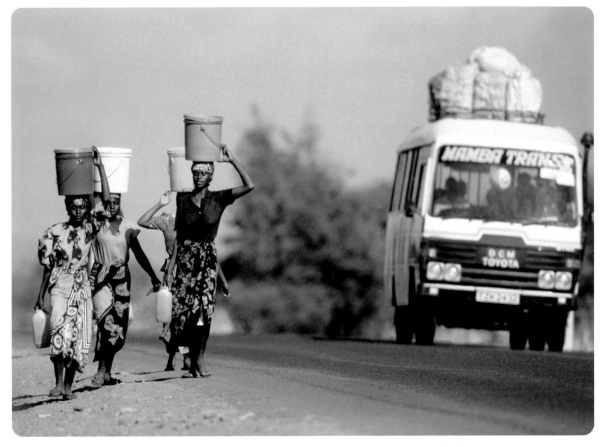

Around the world, billions of people do not have easy access to a water supply for drinking, washing or growing crops, and many have to travel long distances to collect water.

Feeding the World

In 2008, the population of the world was around 6.7 billion. By 2025, it is expected to reach eight billion. This rapidly growing population has placed ever greater demands on supplies of food and water. The impact on the world's resources has been enormous. Forests and wetlands have disappeared, lakes and rivers have been drained, seas and oceans overfished, and grasslands pushed to their limits – all to provide more food and water.

Predicting Disaster

In the late 1960s and early 1970s scientists began to predict a global food crisis that would threaten the lives of hundreds of millions of people. They suggested this would be caused by a rapidly growing population and a shortage of resources to feed them. Although the world population nearly doubled between 1965 and 2005, the predicted global crisis never happened on the scale scientists expected. Instead, developments in food and water technology helped crops to grow, turned deserts into farms and prevented disaster on a massive scale.

In the early years of the twenty-first century, scientists once again began talking about a food and water crisis. The growing population is still blamed as a factor but there are other reasons now, including climate change, poor farming methods and a world trading system that many people think is unfair to several countries. In early 2008 there were food-price riots in a number of countries, including Bangladesh, Egypt and Haiti, and some people think riots like these are signs of this emerging disaster. But what is the real evidence for a twenty-first century crisis, and what is being done to solve the problem in a sustainable way?

Students in Haiti, in the Caribbean, riot in protest against rising food prices. Around 80 per cent of the population in Haiti lives in poverty.

Measurements of Success

Although the rise in the world's population has had a negative impact on the environment and resources (see pages 12–13), the priority to produce more food and water has been largely successful. One way of measuring how successful it has been is to look at global calorie intake – the number of calories (energy from food) that each person receives on average per day. In the early 1960s this was around 2,280 calories per person per day. By 2007, it had increased to 2,800 calories per person per day. In the same period, the number of people who lived in countries where the calorie intake was usually low had fallen. Today, less than 10 per cent of the population lives in countries where the average calorie intake is less than 2,200 per person.

There have also been big improvements in the number of people who have access to enough water, particularly in India and parts of Africa. For example, in India in 1970, only 17 per cent of the population had access to a safe water supply. By 2002, that had increased dramatically – to 86 per cent of the population.

TAKE ACTION

There are many ways that people can help save water. These include:

- Turning off the tap when brushing your teeth.
- Taking a shower instead of a bath.
- Fitting a water meter to pay for the water used and to encourage efficiency.
- Collecting rainwater for watering gardens.
- Only using a washing machine or dishwasher when it is full.
- Washing food in a bowl of water instead of under a running tap.
- Fixing leaky taps to avoid wasting water.
- Fitting a low-flush toilet or putting a water-filled plastic bottle in the toilet cistern to reduce the amount of water used.

CASE STUDY

Ghana: Water Policies

In the 1970s the people of Ghana in West Africa suffered severely from a lack of safe water supplies, particularly in rural areas. Since that time the government and a number of international organisations have made efforts to create sustainable policies that will allow many more people access to water. In towns and cities, water facilities such as treatment plants have been modernised and improved. The Oxfam Water for Survival programme has worked with a local organisation, Rural Aid, to help dig wells and provide pumps for people who live in villages, so they do not have to walk long distances to fetch clean water. In 2008 the National Water Policy was introduced, aiming to further improve the situation in Ghana. Already, 76 per cent of the population has access to clean, safe water supplies.

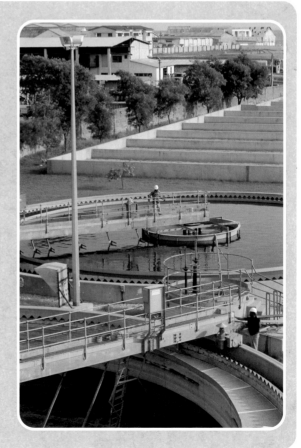

This sewage-treatment plant in Ghana separates solid from liquid waste. The liquid is then purified so it can be safely returned to rivers and used again.

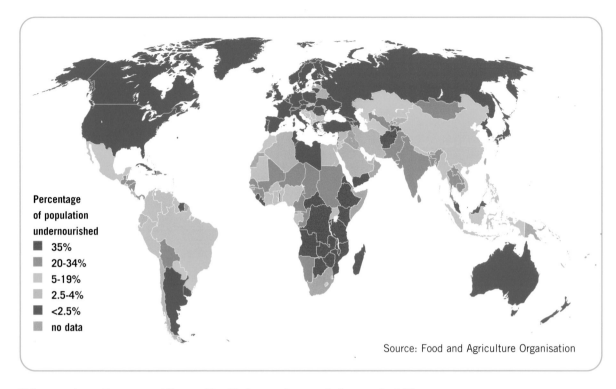

Percentage
of population
undernourished
■ 35%
■ 20-34%
   5-19%
   2.5-4%
■ <2.5%
   no data

Source: Food and Agriculture Organisation

This map shows the areas of the world suffering most severely from malnutrition.

Still Not Enough...

Although many more people now have access
to enough food and water than they did half a
century ago, the problem has not been solved.
Seventeen per cent of the world population –
around 1.1 billion people – still do not have access
to safe water supplies and around one in seven
people go to bed hungry every night. More
importantly, the progress made during the last
half century may be slowing down. In 2006
the United Nations Food and Agricultural
Organisation (FAO) compiled a report which
suggested that the number of malnourished
people actually increased from 823 million to
830 million between 1990 and 2004. Most of
these people lived in sub-Saharan Africa. There
is very little rainfall here, so water supplies are
limited and not enough crops can grow. Growth
in world agriculture is also expected to slow down
considerably in the next 40 years – and if there is
less land being farmed, there is less food available.

...In the Right Place

In 2008, the number of people in the world
suffering from malnutrition was greater than the
population of all the countries in the European
Union and the United States put together. Although
there is enough food in the world to feed everyone,
the problem is that it is not distributed equally.
The average person living in the United States, for
example, has a calorie intake more than twice that
of someone living in the Democratic Republic of
Congo. But malnourishment is not just about
calories, it is also about the balance and quality of
diet. People who get all their calories from just one
food type are still at risk of malnutrition.

Food Distribution and Diet

It is important to understand the problem of
food distribution because as the food and farming
industries become more global, the the quality of
people's diets is affected as well as the total amount
of food available. For example, a farmer in Kenya

decide that instead of growing vegetables to feed himself and his family, he will grow them to be exported to supermarkets in MEDCs. This means that he will have to buy food for himself because he is no longer growing it for personal consumption. As many farmers are now exporting their vegetables, they are in short supply in Kenya and so it is expensive for the farmer to buy them. He may not be able to afford vegetables and will have to buy cheaper food such as maize or beans instead, which do not have the same amount of vitamins and minerals as vegetables. The farmer's diet becomes poorer because of the export trade.

It is clear that providing food for everyone is a complicated issue. Shipping surplus food from one part of the world to another might provide some answers, but it will not meet the need for everyone to have a healthy and balanced diet.

This Somalian boy is suffering from malnutrition. Thousands of people died from the condition during a famine in the country in the 1990s.

FACTS IN FOCUS
Malnutrition

Malnutrition is a medical condition in which people do not have enough nutrients in their diet for their bodies to function properly. People suffering from malnutrition will have very little energy. They are more likely to become ill or catch diseases. Malnutrition can even lead to death. The World Health Organisation has stated that malnutrition is a more serious threat to the world's public health than any disease. It affects people of all ages, but children are the largest group suffering from malnutrition, most of them living in Asia and Africa.

EXPERT VIEW

'Malnutrition is estimated to contribute to more than one-third of all child deaths, although it is rarely listed as the direct cause. Lack of access to highly nutritious foods, especially in the present context of rising food prices, is a common cause of malnutrition.'
WORLD HEALTH ORGANISATION

Fishermen sort and pack fish from a trawler. Fish stocks are under threat as the fishing industry expands.

Overfishing

Many experts believe we are approaching a breaking point in food and water supplies. They argue that even if we are able to increase the amount of food being produced, the environment would not be able to cope. An example of this problem is fish stocks. As more and more fish are being caught to provide food for the growing global population, stocks of some fish, including cod and sole, have dropped to dangerously low levels in certain areas. There is a risk that some species will die out, or their numbers will be so much reduced that there is no longer enough to feed people. The reduction in fish stocks is not only caused by overfishing, though. Other factors have also contributed, including pollution, climate change and 'bycatch' (see Facts in Focus).

Laws limiting the numbers of species that can be caught are a step towards reversing the damage to fish stocks, but there are other solutions. Marine reserves can be established – areas where no fishing is allowed at all. One-third of the Great Barrier Reef in Australia is now a marine reserve, for example, and sea life there is increasing. People could also stop buying fish that are under threat.

Soil Erosion

In agriculture, too, there are signs that the environment cannot cope with demand. Crop yields in many areas are declining as soils lose

FACTS IN FOCUS
Bycatch

Bycatch is marine creatures that are caught by accident by fishing trawlers. Sometimes the fish are the right species but they are too young and small to be sold. Around half the cod and haddock caught in the North Sea, for example, are thrown back into the water, dead or dying. Some bycatch is fish of the wrong species. The shrimp industry has the worst record – up to 80 per cent of the species caught in shrimp nets is bycatch. Bycatch can also include marine mammals like whales and dolphins. They usually die before they can be released back into the sea. Some fishing boats now have special escape hatches that force the whale or dolphin out of the net and back into the sea.

their fertility from being farmed too intensively. Farmers keep up production by applying more and more fertiliser, but this can end up contaminating local water supplies. In countries like Brazil, areas of forest have been cut down to make way for farmland, and natural vegetation has been removed so crops can be grown. These activities have also led to soil erosion.

There are a number of sustainable solutions to the problem of soil erosion. One of the most effective systems is called 'crop rotation'. Planting the same crop in a particular field every year can reduce the nutrients in the soil, resulting in soil erosion, so many farmers now change the crops they plant in a field each year.

Water for Food Production

Seventy per cent of the world's freshwater is used for agriculture, but increased population, polluted supplies and environmental changes are leading to

Contour farming can limit the amounts of freshwater used for irrigation. Fields are ploughed along the lines of the slope, which slows down rainwater runoff.

shortages of freshwater. Shifts in agricultural production, changes to the global trade system (see pages 36-37), and improvements in farm technology and water efficiency are all seen as potential solutions to the current challenges.

CASE STUDY

Central Asia: The Aral Sea

The Aral Sea in Central Asia is a dramatic example of what happens when people do not consider the longer-term effects of crop production. Large amounts of water for irrigation were diverted from the rivers that ran into the Aral Sea – so much so that by 2007 it was only one-tenth of its original size. Dam projects are now underway to try and reverse the damage and start restoring the sea. Other suggestions have been made, including pumping water from the Caspian Sea into the Aral basin and diverting water from other rivers in the region. These are all expensive solutions, but they could save the sea within two or three decades.

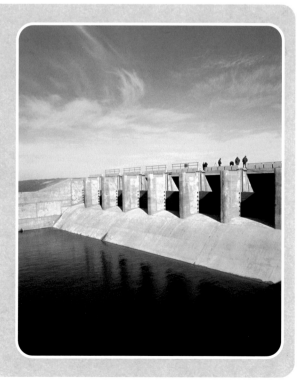

A 13-km-long dam has been built to keep in the water that is now returning to the Aral basin.

Competing Needs

Meeting basic human needs is not the only pressure on food and water supplies across the world. Water is needed for industry, domestic use and for generating electricity in the form of hydroelectric power (HEP). The land available for farming is also needed for growing crops that can generate biofuels, and to house the growing world population. The competition for water and land resources presents a great challenge – which options provide the most sustainable solutions?

Urbanisation

Urbanisation is the process in which more and more people are moving to towns and cities around the world. In 2007, for the first time in history, more people lived in towns than in the countryside. By 2050, experts predict that more than 70 per cent of the population will live in towns. As cities expand to cope with the numbers of people settling in them, more water is needed to support the growing populations and more land is needed to build places for them to live. Farmland is taken over by building developments. This is called 'urban sprawl'.

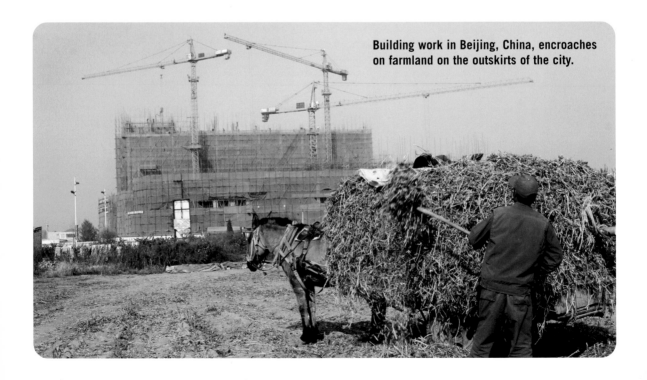

Building work in Beijing, China, encroaches on farmland on the outskirts of the city.

In Malaysia, farmers like this are in short supply because so many people have moved from the countryside to the cities.

EXPERT VIEW

'Small farmers produce much of the developing world's food. Yet they are generally much poorer than the rest of the population in these countries… Dealing with poverty and hunger … means confronting the problems that small farmers and their families face in their daily struggle for survival.'
FOOD AND AGRICULTURE ORGANISATION, *FARMING SYSTEMS AND POVERTY*

Many cities were built in areas where food production was high and water supplies were good – both reasons for locating there. As farmland is taken over by developments, food production is pushed on to less fertile or drier land. This reduces the amount and quality of the food produced, and standards of living in the area drop. The competing needs of urbanisation and agriculture for both land and water is already a big challenge for governments.

Rural to Urban Migration

Big cities often attract people from rural areas because they offer opportunities for higher incomes and better services such as education and healthcare facilities. This movement from villages to towns is called 'rural to urban migration'. A study by the United Nations predicts that half of all urban population growth up to 2025 will be as a result of rural to urban migration. This could mean up to 1.1 billion people – almost all of them in less economically developed countries (LEDCs) – leaving the countryside. Without people to work on the farms, less food is being produced. In Malaysia, for example, around 730,000 hectares of farmland are not being used or have unharvested crops, because there are not enough people to work the land. How can people be encouraged to stay in the countryside and farm the land if they feel they will earn more money by moving to towns and cities and working in different industries?

One solution is to improve living standards in rural areas and to offer incentives to farmers to stay on the land. This can be difficult in countries where little money is available, but the World Bank has launched the Rural Development Strategy, which invests in programmes to help poor people in rural areas.

Biofuels

The growth of biofuels is one of the most recent forms of competition for land and water resources to emerge. Biofuels are fuels that are made from plant-based sources, and they are increasingly being used because they are a more environmentally friendly alternative to fossil fuels.

The majority of the world's transportation depends on oil as a fuel source, but oil is also a big contributor to climate change, because when oil-based products like petrol and diesel are burned they release carbon dioxide. Many nations have started to use biofuels instead of oil-based fuels in order to reduce carbon-dioxide emissions. The United Kingdom, for example, has set a target for biofuels to make up at least five per cent of all fuel sold at pumps by 2010, while the United States has set a target of 15 per cent by around 2017. Other countries are making similar commitments, so the demand for biofuels is increasing.

Biofuels and Rising Food Prices

Growing crops that are made into biofuels can provide farmers with a good income, so many farmers are choosing to grow biofuel crops rather than food crops. As more land is given over to biofuel crops, less is available for cultivating food crops. If less food is produced, costs rise. Food prices are increasing all over the world, and many people have blamed biofuels for this. In the European Union, for example, the price of rapeseed oil rose by 63 per cent between 2003 and 2007, mainly due to its increased use as a source of biofuel rather than as a food product.

FACTS IN FOCUS
Rising Food Prices

The World Bank said that average food prices in May 2008 were around 2.5 times higher than in 2002. The organisation is especially concerned about the impact of these price rises in LEDCs, where up to 80 per cent of household income can be spent on food. It has been suggested that up to 100 million people could be plunged back into poverty as a result and that prices are likely to remain high for several years to come.

An bioethanol production plant in the United States. In the USA, 20 per cent of the corn grown is used for bioethanol.

CASE STUDY

Brazil: Ethanol Capital of the World

Brazil first began to use sugar-based ethanol fuels in its vehicles in the 1970s, when oil prices across the world were increasing. Not only was bioethanol cheaper, but it also avoided the risk of fluctuating oil prices that were typical of the 1970s and 1980s. Today, bioethanol fuel is available at around 29,000 filling stations in Brazil and costs around one-third less than petrol. It accounts for about 20 per cent of Brazil's transport fuel market and Brazil even exports it to Sweden and Japan. Brazil has been criticised by environmentalists, who say that as more farmland is used to grow sugar cane to make bioethanol, other farm activities (especially ranching) are pushed further into Brazil's fragile forest and grassland ecosystems. The Brazilian government denies this and continues to expand bioethanol production.

A worker in Brazil harvests sugar cane that will be used to make bioethanol. As more biofuel crops are grown, areas of rainforest are cut down to provide more land for food crops.

Wider Effects of Biofuel Production

There are also concerns about the indirect effects of biofuel production. In the United States, many farmers who had previously grown soya are now growing corn instead. The corn is used to make bioethanol, a biofuel, and this type of farming is supported by government payments called subsidies. As soya farmers in the United States switch to corn, farmers in Brazil are encouraged to grow more soya for export to the United States and elsewhere. They do this by clearing new land in the Amazon rainforest or by taking over pastures and driving cattle ranching further into the forest. This has led to what environmentalists are calling an 'arc of deforestation' in the Amazon region. Some people believe this is linked to the increased demand for biofuels.

Others, however, say that biofuels are not to blame and that rising costs and the expansion of farmland are more to do with higher incomes and changing diets in countries like China and India, both of which would lead to a greater demand for food. Biofuels are an important factor in planning a sustainable future for our environment, but which should take priority – addressing the environmental concerns of climate change, or ensuring that enough food is being grown to feed our growing population?

A Green Revolution

The 'green revolution' is the name given to improvements in agricultural science and technology that have improved food production. In the past, practices such as greater use of irrigation and the development of chemicals that promoted growth and reduced pests have helped avoid hunger on a massive scale. However, more developments are likely to be needed if we are to avoid a future crisis in food production.

Increasing Land Use

One way to increase production is simply to increase areas of farmland and the amount of water used. This has already occurred in many parts of the world, for example in the Philippines and China. Agricultural land now covers 37.5 per cent of the world's land surface. The amount of freshwater being used has also increased, by 325 per cent between 1965 and 2005.

The problem with this expansion of farmland is that it has already destroyed enormous areas of natural habitat. This has had a dramatic impact on wildlife. The populations of many animal species have dropped as habitats are lost to make way for farmland. Expansion has also removed

The increased use of pesticides and chemical fertilisers has improved crop yields.

the important environmental services that these habitats provided. When wetlands are drained for agriculture, for example, they are no longer available to store water, to help with flood control or to provide a place for fish to breed. In the long term this can affect food production because the quality of the remaining water becomes worse, risks of flooding are higher and fish stocks are reduced.

Similar problems can occur when forests are cleared to make way for farmland. For example, forests in the Congo river basin in central Africa play a significant role in the water cycle – the trees store water from rainfall and release it back into the atmosphere through a process called transpiration. Trees recycle between 75 and 95 per cent of rainfall in this area. If the forests are removed this important natural cycle is disrupted.

Improving Efficiency

As more and more natural habitats are destroyed by a range of human activities, the resources available to meet our food and water needs are reduced. To solve this problem a lot of attention is now focused on how we might use resources more efficiently. Intensive farming already means that a lot more food can be produced in a smaller area, but the challenge is how to continue this without damaging the environment.

FACTS IN FOCUS
The Intensification of Global Food Production

Year	Arable land (ha/person)	Cereal yield (kg/ha)
1965	0.35	1,644
1975	0.29	2,101
1985	0.26	2,726
1995	0.25	2,775
2005	0.22	3,254

Source: World Development Indicators 2008

Rice terraces in the Philippines. The amount of land used for agriculture in the country increased from 81,320 sq km in 1965 to 122,000 sq km by 2005.

EXPERT VIEW

'Needed for the twenty-first century is a ... doubly green revolution in agricultural technology. Productivity increases are still vital, but must be combined with environmental protection or restoration, while new technologies must be both affordable by, and geared to the needs of, the poor and undernourished.'

FOOD AND AGRICULTURE ORGANISATION, *WORLD AGRICULTURE: TOWARDS 2015/2030*

Irrigation

Irrigation is used to provide water for crops in areas where there is very little rainfall, or where rainfall is unpredictable. The water for irrigation can be diverted from rivers or lakes, captured or harvested in reservoirs, or pumped from groundwater sources. Across the world, the area of irrigated farmland increased from 149 million hectares in 1965 to over 280 million hectares by 2008. Irrigation has played an important role in improving methods of farming, and many experts see it as an essential part of any further improvements.

There are three main types of irrigation: surface irrigation, sprinkler irrigation and drip irrigation. They have different levels of efficiency based on how much water is wasted in the process.

Surface Irrigation

In surface irrigation water is allowed to flood the surface of a field. The water normally reaches the field through a channel with a gate in it, but it can also be pumped on to the field. Surface irrigation is the least efficient kind – up to 60 per cent of the water is wasted. It simply runs off the ground or sinks in without benefiting plant growth.

Sprinkler Irrigation

In sprinkler irrigation water is sprayed in the air to simulate rainfall. Up to 30 per cent of water is wasted through evaporation from leaves, by overshooting the field or through over-watering on the ground.

Sprinkler irrigation uses a system of hoses, pipes and sprinklers to spray water in the air so it falls on the crops like rainfall. Sometimes a pump is needed.

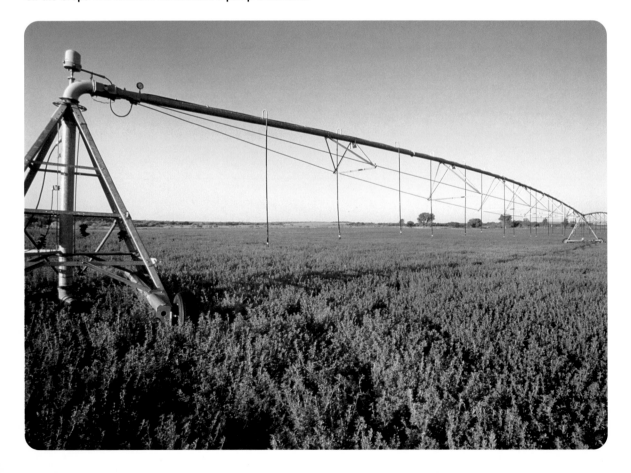

Drip Irrigation

In drip irrigation, small quantities of water are carried in pipes with small holes that allow water to be released close to the crop roots. Only around 10 per cent of water is wasted and over-watering is less likely because water is delivered more directly.

Crop Yields

In general, more efficient irrigation results in more crops. Unfortunately, the most efficient systems are also the most expensive so they tend to be used for crops that have a high value or for non-food crops like cut flowers. Improving irrigation systems so that more food crops can be grown is important for three key reasons:

- Irrigated farmland is up to three times more productive than land that relies on rainfall. In 2008, irrigated farmland accounted for around 17 per cent of the world's cropland, but produced 40 per cent of the global harvest.

- Each calorie of food produced requires about one litre of water. Limited water supplies are reducing the amount of food being produced, so irrigation systems that use less water for the same result will benefit food production.

- Inefficient irrigation can cause salinisation – where surplus water evaporates or raises the water table (the level of water underground) to contaminate the soil with mineral salts that are in the water.

In 2008 only around one per cent of irrigated land was managed using the most efficient systems, but these reduced water use by at least 60 per cent. The FAO has been experimenting with low-cost drip-irrigation systems that use simple filters and a low-pressure system instead of expensive pumps. These have helped farmers in LEDCs to reduce water use or increase the area cultivated for the same amount of water as before.

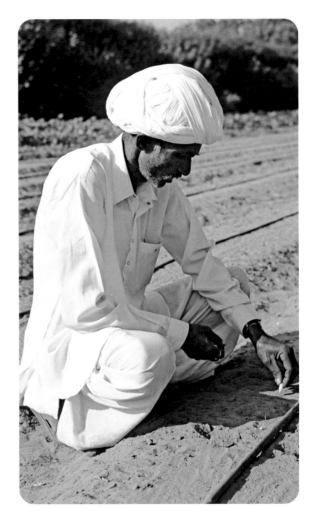

A farmer plants garlic next to drip-irrigation pipes in northern India. Drip irrigation delivers water directly to plant roots, limiting water waste.

EXPERT VIEW

'Water, mixed with fertiliser, is pumped through the pipes and comes out here, drop by drop, right by the plant's root. With the same amount of water, this system allows us to double or triple the surface cultivated. Even with less rain, it allows you to irrigate. It means that we can be a lot less dependant on the heavens!'

MARIA HELENA SEMEDO, FAO'S REPRESENTATIVE TO NIGER, DESCRIBING THE BENEFITS OF DRIP IRRIGATION

In countries like Afghanistan, new varieties of crops such as wheat that give a higher yield have dramatically improved food production and helped avoid a crisis in basic food supplies.

Biotechnology

Irrigation provides just one way of increasing food supplies. Other technologies are available that also offer the potential for meeting the world's food needs in a sustainable way. Biotechnology (plant science) in particular could hold the key to avoiding a global crisis – but it also raises many questions. In the 1960s, the green revolution looked at plant science as a way of increasing food supplies by creating high-yield varieties (HYVs) of staple crops such as rice and wheat. These new varieties allowed countries on the brink of famine, such as Mexico, India and Pakistan, to grow enough food to feed their populations.

The downside to these so-called 'miracle crops' was that they required a whole package of other technologies to maximise their effect, including irrigation, fertilisers and pesticides. All these factors increased the cost for farmers. Many could not afford the package and ended up losing their land to wealthier landlords. A lack of training also meant that the use of chemicals was often inaccurate, leading to pollution of the local environment and particularly water supplies. Many farmers also failed to wear protective clothing when working with the chemicals, which caused them health problems.

Genetically Modified Foods

A new era of biotechnology is now providing breakthroughs that go far beyond breeding high-yield varieties and actually look at engineering new species. Genetic modification (GM) is a process that allows scientists to identify the individual genes that make up all life on Earth and artificially adapt them in plants and animals. Crops can be genetically modified to improve their resistance to certain pests, for example, or to require less water they can be grown in semi-arid (dry) regions. Supporters of GM technology believe it may hold the key to avoiding a global food crisis by increasing yields, raising farm incomes, reducing chemical use and conserving water. They claim GM crops are better for the environment and can even improve human health by processes such as enriching rice with beta-carotene to increase the production of Vitamin A. Vitamin A deficiency causes blindness in 500,000 children and up to two million deaths every year.

EXPERT VIEW

'I am in favour of careful use of this technology rather than careless rejection. Equally I am not claiming that the only choice is between adoption of genetically modified crops and mass starvation… We should use whatever we have.'

MARTIN WOLF, JOURNALIST AND ECONOMICS EDITOR

FACTS IN FOCUS
Top 10 GM Food Producers

Rank	Country	GM Crop Area (million ha)	Total Crop Area (million ha)
1	USA	54.6	118.6
2	Argentina	18.0	32.3
3	Brazil	11.5	64.2
4	Canada	6.1	27.09
5	India	3.8	199.7
6	China	3.5	176.1
7	Paraguay	2.0	4.5
8	South Africa	1.4	5.05
9	Uruguay	0.4	0.95
10	Philippines	0.2	12.9

Source: Friends of the Earth International, 2008

Some experts believe that GM food will reduce the amount of chemicals used in farming and limit the risk of pollution to water supplies.

The Problems with GM

GM technology is controlled by a handful of very large companies, which can make large profits from selling GM seeds. There is concern that GM crops will not help the millions of small-scale farmers who need to improve their food supplies. Instead it could put them at risk of price rises beyond their control. Another concern with GM is that 'playing with nature' could have unknown outcomes if GM varieties contaminate natural varieties or affect the health of wildlife and even humans. These reasons have led several nations to ban GM crops until they are better understood. In many countries the public are so against the use of GM crops that many supermarkets have adopted labelling schemes to prove that foods are GM free.

Perhaps the biggest concern with GM crops, however, is that in many cases they have not so far improved food supplies as people hoped. Studies of GM soya production in the United States, for example, have shown that harvests of GM soya

EXPERT VIEW

'Who wants to eat a crop that kills pests who try to eat it? It's not natural. No one I know likes the idea.'

LI MING FU, FARMER IN XISHUANGBANNA VILLAGE, SOUTHERN YUNNAN PROVINCE, CHINA

can be between six and 10 per cent lower than non-GM soya. Furthermore, they have only been successful in competing with non-GM varieties where larger amounts of chemicals are used. The seed companies producing GM crops argue against this, and several countries are still carrying out experiments with GM varieties, but it seems that we cannot fully rely on them to meet future needs.

Copying Nature

The opposite to GM technology is to work with and copy nature. Our planet's natural environments are extremely diverse and highly productive, and

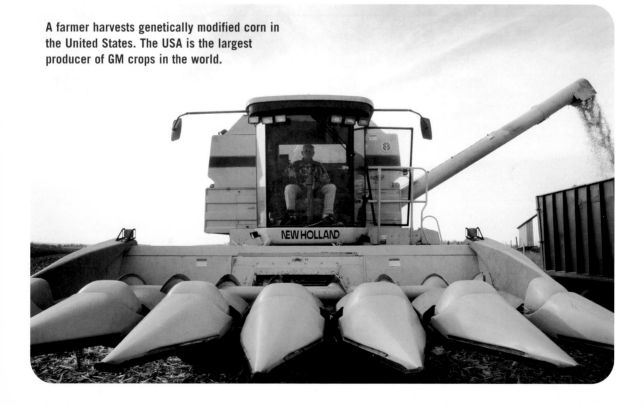

A farmer harvests genetically modified corn in the United States. The USA is the largest producer of GM crops in the world.

many scientists believe we could learn a great deal more from them. Organic farming is one method that attempts to do this by reducing the use of artificial chemicals and instead using natural fertilisers and pest control (see pages 26–27).

There are also changes in farming practice that copy nature, such as growing trees and food crops together in a practice known as agroforestry or silviculture. Agroforestry has been shown to increase yields and can also provide many environmental benefits, such as blocking harmful winds, reducing soil erosion and conserving water supplies.

Another lesson from nature is to combine fishing and farming. This has been done very successfully in parts of China by raising fish in paddy fields planted with rice (see page 31). There may also be new varieties of staple crops such as maize and rice that could increase yields of cultivated varieties.

Agroforestry involves planting crops among existing forest areas. It prevents soil erosion and deforestation.

CASE STUDY

Bolivia: Agroforestry

Farmers in the Yungas region of Bolivia rely on crops such as citrus fruit, coffee and cocoa for their livelihoods. Until recently the slash-and-burn farming technique was used, in which trees were cut down and the remains burned to clear plots for farming. Even when the land was cleared it could be up to four years before farmers had a harvestable crop. Slash and burn causes soil erosion so after a few years farmers would have to move on to a new plot, which caused further deforestation.

In the early 2000s, the Yungas Community Alternative Development Fund (YCADF) began working with farmers on agroforestry methods, planting crops alongside trees. Nutrients in the soil are retained so the plot can be farmed for many years. Agroforestry also results in a harvestable crop in the first year of planting. It has provided farmers with a sustainable income, using sustainable methods that do not harm the environment.

Sustainable Solutions

With concerns growing about the environmental impact of some methods of increasing food and water supplies, there is now a major effort to find more sustainable solutions. The challenge is to improve the supply and availability of food and water without damaging the environment or using up resources for future generations. Organic farming is one of the better-known sustainable solutions, but there are others that focus on either food or water – or, better still, on ways of using food and water together in a sustainable way.

Organic Farming

Before the invention of artificial chemicals, food was grown using the nutrients and defences that were found in nature – a method broadly known as organic farming. In recent years organic farming has become more popular again, as a way of addressing concerns about levels of food production and other issues such as the use of chemicals in farming. Farmers, politicians and consumers have all realised that although chemical farming may be more productive, the damage it causes to the environment and the additional cost in energy and resources such as fossil fuels make it highly unsustainable. Many people see

A mother and her children farm organic crops in Uganda.

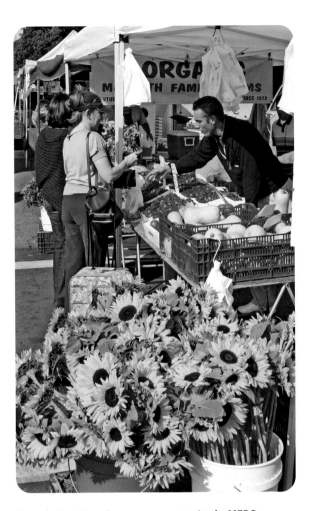

Organic food has become very popular in MEDCs, where people can afford to pay higher prices. Local farmers grow their produce and sell it at markets.

organic farming as a sustainable alternative to chemical farming and it is a fast-growing method of agriculture. Organic methods of farming are regulated internationally by the International Federation of Organic Agriculture Movements.

The Cost of Organic Food

One of the key problems with organic farming is that it requires a lot more time and skill than non-organic farming, and many of these skills have been lost during the switch to chemical farming. It takes more time to grow organic crops, and the yields are lower, both of which make organic food more expensive to buy. In fact, this additional cost is exaggerated because the true costs of non-organic produce, such as the environmental damage it causes, are not taken into consideration. Organic food has also become fashionable and is promoted by celebrity chefs and high-profile campaign groups as being better for human health as well as the environment. Like many fashionable items, this means consumers can be charged more because of high demand for the products.

Organically grown beans being packed in Kenya. These will be shipped around the world, so the environmental cost of transportation must be weighed against the benefits of organic growing methods.

Organic Challenges

Besides the lower productivity and higher costs, organic farming faces other challenges. Firstly, for food to qualify as organic the land it is produced on must be certified as organic. It can take several years for land that was farmed with chemicals to return to organic status, and in areas where organic land is close to non-organic land there is a risk that crops could be contaminated by chemicals used on the non-organic land.

A second challenge is the supply of organic produce. The fastest-growing demand is in the wealthier markets of Europe and North America, but these countries do not have enough organic land to meet demand and so they import large quantities of organic food. The energy needed to transport this food, together with the carbon emissions it generates, often outweigh the environmental benefits of growing organic produce in the first place.

A third challenge is that organic farming methods are more labour-intensive. In the United Kingdom there is evidence that this has been a positive factor and helped to provide new farming jobs in an industry where 80 per cent of jobs had been lost since the 1960s. Where there is still a rapid movement of workers from rural to urban areas, however, there may not be enough people to meet the increased labour needs of growing food organically.

Pick and Mix

Replacing chemical-based farming with organic farming may help to reduce the pressure on resources and protect the environment, but if it is to play a key role in the future of food production it must be shown to actively increase the amount of food provided. A solution to this might be combining some of the principles of organic farming with other farming methods in a sort of pick-and-mix system. An example of this is the System of Rice Intensification (SRI), which combines methods of using land, seeds, water, nutrients and human labour. The SRI method follows many organic principles, such as the use of compost and manure rather than chemicals as fertilisers. The method also minimises the use of water by keeping the plant roots moist rather than flooding the whole field, as in conventional rice paddies.

SRI rice can use 25–50 per cent less water than conventional methods – which is extremely important for the millions of people who live in areas short of water and who rely on rice as their staple food. The most important impact, however, is the increase in yields. Whether using traditional or hybrid varieties of rice, farmers have reported increased yields of 20–40 per cent when using SRI instead of conventional methods. When combined with a lower environmental impact and reduced use of water, energy and resources, this makes SRI one of the most significant breakthroughs in sustainable agriculture in recent years. If SRI was used on 20 million hectares of land under rice cultivation in India, for example, experts have predicted that India would meet its 2050 target for increased grain production as early as 2012.

EXPERT VIEW

'The System of Rice Intensification improves yields with less water, less seed, and less chemical inputs than most conventional methods of rice cultivation. This means that the returns on inputs are higher, making the method potentially more profitable than most of the traditional methods. SRI is ideal in giving impoverished rural communities the much-needed food and health security, while conserving scarce natural resources, particularly water.'

WWF, *MORE RICE WITH LESS WATER*, 2007

As the food crisis worsens in LEDCs such as India, more farmers are turning to SRI to increase yields.

CASE STUDY

Madagascar: Rice Intensification

The System of Rice Intensification began in Madagascar in the 1980s, and its effects are now fully being felt in its country of origin. Over the past five years Madagascan farmers have reported that using this system has increased their rice yields more than fourfold. This is particularly important in countries like Madagascar, which cannot afford many of the technologies being developed in other parts of the world to help improve their crop output. There are now programmes being introduced to expand the use of SRI to more parts of Madagascar and it has provided a model for several other countries. In total, 28 countries were introducing SRI in 2008, including China, India and Indonesia – with a combined population of 2.7 billion.

Urban Agriculture

Urbanisation (see page 14) places great pressure on food and water resources, but it can also provide opportunities. In many countries, people moving from the countryside to urban areas bring farming skills with them, and it is possible to find small pockets of farming in even the largest cities. This 'urban agriculture' makes use of vacant land to grow vegetables or fruit crops; of the city fringes to grow cereals; and of backyards to keep a few chickens or a pig, cow or goat.

Urban agriculture can improve diets and provide a source of income for people who live in cities. However, there is a danger that it can become a health hazard. Pollution from untreated waste, for example, can contaminate the land and water used for urban agriculture. Sometimes too many pesticides are used in urban plots, and the chemicals in the pesticides can get into drinking-water supplies. A 2003 study of *palak* (spinach) sold in Delhi, India, found that virtually all of it failed to meet national health guidelines.

Several cities are now recognising the importance of urban agriculture and introducing planning and monitoring to better support and control it. In the Cuban capital, Havana, there are more than 20,000 small plots covering some 2,770 hectares that are farmed by Havana's residents. These are vital to local food production and are strictly monitored by the city authorities to ensure they are safe for consumers.

Reusing Water for Farming

Recycling treated waste water for use in irrigation is a sustainable option with enormous potential benefits to both food and water supplies, especially in light of our rapidly urbanising world. A city with a population of 500,000 and water consumption of 120 litres per person a day produces about 48,000 cubic metres of waste

A man works in his urban plot in the Cuban capital Havana.

CASE STUDY

China: Rice-Fish Farming

In parts of China, farmers have been raising fish in their rice paddies for many years, and this has proven to be very sustainable. It increases yields of both fish and rice, and reduces the use of chemicals. The fish eat weeds that would otherwise compete with rice for growing space, and their waste provides a natural fertiliser that boosts rice growth. Rice-fish farming also uses water more efficiently by producing rice and fish from the same water. Across China, rice yields increase by around 11 per cent when cultivated with fish, and each hectare of rice paddy can produce between 150 and 450 kg of fish a year. There are human benefits too, including less need for weeding, improved diet with a regular source of protein, and an additional source of income from selling fish.

China has over 1.5 million hectares of land under rice-fish farming, and other countries are now expanding their use of this technique.

water every day. When treated, this waste water could be used to irrigate around 500 hectares. The nutrients in the waste are almost as valuable as the water itself! The amount of waste from normal sewage could provide all the nitrogen and much of the phosphorus and potassium normally required for agricultural crop production.

This sewage-treatment plant separates the waste from water and recycles it. The recycled water can be used to water crops.

Grow Your Own

It is possible for individuals to grow their own food, even where there is not much space. Many food crops can be grown in small containers and even indoors. People with gardens could consider using part of their plot to grow their own food. Digging up lawns in favour of food crops could dramatically alter food production – as was proven during the 'Dig for Victory' campaign of the Second World War. By the end of the war in 1945, Britain had some 1.5 million allotments, producing around 10 per cent of the country's food.

With rising oil prices, growing food shortages and greater concerns about where our food comes from, many people believe growing our own food will become more popular in the future and that gardens may soon be feeding their owners. China, Japan, Argentina, Kenya, and South Africa are among countries similarly promoting urban agriculture as a sustainable solution to urban food needs.

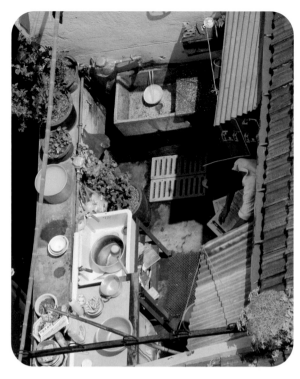

A small rooftop garden in Shanghai. The Chinese government plans to develop 930,000 square metres of urban rooftop gardens by 2018.

CASE STUDY

Canada: SkyFarm

An ambitious scientist in Toronto, Canada, has made plans to use a system of growing food in nutrient-rich water (rather than soil) called hydroponics to produce a vertical SkyFarm in the middle of a city. This would be a 58-floor building using recycled water to grow enough food in the heart of Toronto to feed 35,000 people every day! The SkyFarm reduces the environmental impact of having to transport food from outside areas into the city, and because it is a method of indoor farming, the success of crops does not depend on unpredictable weather. Other countries, including the United States, are planning more systems of 'vertical farming'.

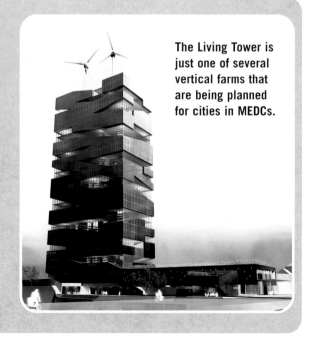

The Living Tower is just one of several vertical farms that are being planned for cities in MEDCs.

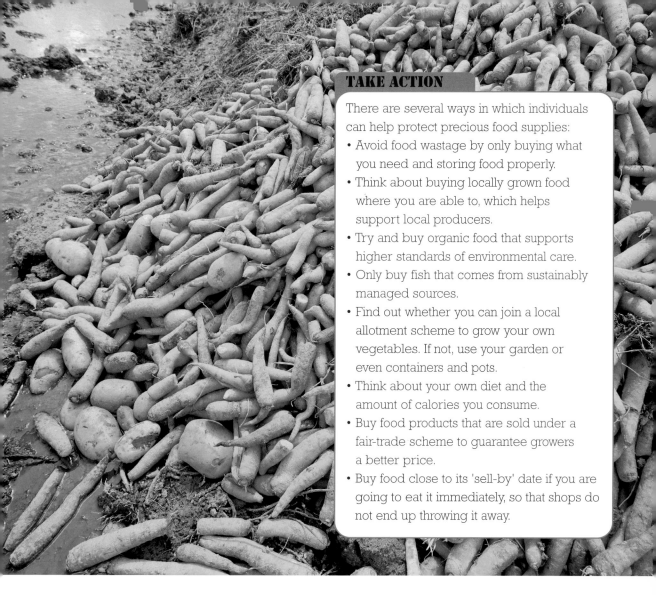

Carrots and potatoes spill out of a commercial waste dump. The amount of food that is thrown away in MEDCs is a big concern when seen in the context of the global food crisis.

Reducing Waste

Wasting food and water reduces the sustainability of any practice. Reducing the amount of water lost through leaky pipes and collecting as much as possible from rainwater or greywater recycling (reusing water used from washing, for example) would all contribute to greater sustainability. In Sydney, Australia, waste water is being treated and reprocessed for use in watering gardens and washing cars. This reduces the use of drinking water for such purposes and helps conserve water resources in one of the driest regions of the world.

In the United States it is estimated that between 25 and 50 per cent of all food ends up being thrown away. The UN World Food Programme has said that surplus food from the USA could feed every hungry person in Africa. If it had not been produced and sold to MEDCs in the first place, the food itself and the water used in its cultivation may have benefited LEDCs. Of course, some of it is thrown because it goes out of date or is half eaten. Those who sell the food and those who buy it could reduce the amount that is sold and bought to prevent it becoming unwanted waste in the future.

Trade and Distribution

No matter how productive and sustainable food and water production become, the world still faces the problem of a mismatch between supply and demand. The trade and distribution of both are therefore just as important to consider in striving for development without damage. Food is one of the most widely traded products in the world, so this is far from simple, but there are ways of improving the trade and distribution of food.

The World Food Trade

Trade in food has taken place for thousands of years, but until quite recently it was on a relatively limited scale. Modern storage and transportation technologies allowed a significant increase in food trade during the second half of the last century, and they far outpaced any increase in food production. Trade in cereals, for example, increased by 251 per cent between 1961 and 1999, but production increased by only 137 per cent. The amount of meat traded increased by 500 per cent over the same period compared to a production increase of 222 per cent. These patterns are repeated for trade in vegetable oils, milk, and vegetables and fruit.

Globalisation

What these figures mean is that food circulates around the world more than ever before, as part of a process known as globalisation. The result of this is that there are more people involved in the food-supply chain. At one time food may have passed directly from farmer to consumer through a local farmers' market, but today it is increasingly likely that consumers buy food from a supermarket or other retailer. They in turn may buy from a

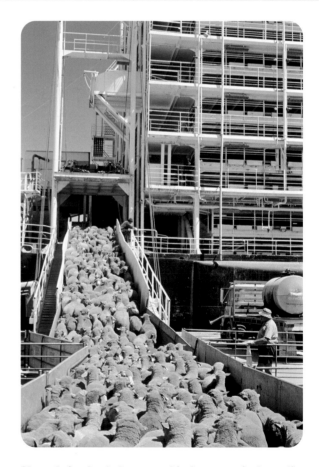

Sheep being loaded on to a ship for export in Australia. The globalisation of the food industry has improved the economies of several nations, but has also had a negative impact for many small farmers.

wholesaler, who buys from an importer, who buys from a stock agent, who may finally buy from the farmer.

With so many people in the chain, the money paid for the final product has to be split between all those involved. The parties at the end of the chain, such as the supermarkets selling to you, have much greater power than the farmers at the beginning of the chain. Their buying decisions affect the whole chain and determine what prices farmers will finally receive for their produce. In the United States, for example, for every US$1 spent on food, only around US$0.19 goes to the farmer – the rest is divided amongst those further down the chain.

EXPERT VIEW

'The distance between producer and consumer has grown ever wider as world trade in food has increased. Food-supply chains have become longer and more complicated, and consumers are often unaware of the source of the food they eat, the conditions for the workers who produce the food, and the environmental impact of its production, processing, packaging and distribution.'

THE EARTHSCAN ATLAS OF FOOD

Buyers inspect frozen tuna fish at a wholesalers in Tokyo, Japan. Wholesalers are one link in a long chain of food-industry contributors.

Changing Prices

Supermarkets and others at the end of the chain work in a competitive environment and want to keep prices as low as possible to attract customers. This creates a downward pressure on the price of food, which means that over time farmers have received less and less for their produce. The cost of major food commodities (wheat, rice, coffee, tea, cocoa, sugar, maize, etc.) fell more or less consistently in the second half of the last century. By 2002–03 many were trading at lower prices than they had been 20 years before. Since 2003, the price of many commodities has increased because there is a greater demand for them from rapidly developing economies such as India and China. The growing demand for biofuels and the increased amount of processed foods in our diets is also causing food prices to rise.

These increased prices have benefited many large-scale commercial farmers in countries such as Canada, Brazil, Argentina, Australia and the United States, but for many of the world's poorest people it has simply meant an increase in the cost of food. By 2008 food prices faced additional pressures as global oil prices hit record highs.

Huge farms in countries like Canada benefit from the worldwide increase in food prices, but small farmers in LEDCs suffer badly from the same phenomenon.

In an era of a global food markets, this increase is passed on throughout the supply chain, as each part of the chain has to pay more in energy and transportation costs.

Changing the Rules

In June 2008, the United Nations held a conference to discuss the problem of rising food prices and warned of a major crisis unless there was not only an increase in production, but also a change in the way that food is traded. At the moment, trade is dominated by a relatively small number of hugely influential countries. Many of these are protected by tax systems that pay subsidies to their own farmers, whilst charging tariffs on food imported from other countries.

Such systems protect local farming, but have a dramatic impact on world trade because they allow farmers to produce food for less than the true market value (because they are being paid a guaranteed subsidy). This increased production lowers world prices and means farmers growing food in countries without subsidies can see their incomes fall. Subsidies can also influence what is grown. Subsidies on biofuel crops have reduced the area used to produce food, for example, and some say this is at least partly to blame for the food shortages and rising prices in 2007–08.

The subsidies paid to farmers in MEDCs totalled around US$300 billion in 2008. The impact of this is more clearly seen when you consider that just one week's worth of these subsidies would meet the cost of providing food aid to all the world's hungry for an entire year. Scrapping the subsidies may help to free up the world food market and give farmers in LEDCs better opportunities to sell their produce.

The United Nations conference in 2008 addressed the problems of rising food prices.

FACTS IN FOCUS
Agricultural Subsidies

Agricultural subsidies are money paid by governments to farmers to supplement their income. Crop yields can vary depending on factors such as weather conditions, so a farmer's income can change dramatically from year to year. Subsidies mean that farmers have a guaranteed income even in years where crop yields are low. Many people argue that subsidies work against the idea of free trade. Often only wealthier countries can afford to pay subsidies, which means that farmers in poorer countries suffer because they cannot produce crops at competitive prices. Do countries have the right to protect their own farmers, or should there be one law that applies to all and keeps prices the same all over the world?

Fair Trade

One response to existing trade patterns is the fair-trade movement. This guarantees farmers a minimum price for their produce that is set above the long-term market average. Farmers can earn up to double the market value during times when prices are low, and if prices rise then farmers are paid at the market rate. The most important aspect of fair trade, however, is that the guaranteed price allows farmers to plan ahead, and they are often paid a share of the money in advance so that they can invest properly in their activities. To qualify for fair-trade certification farmers must also show that they are adopting sustainable practices – that they are farming in a way that protects the environment and invests in the local community.

The fair-trade movement began in the Netherlands, but has since spread to many other countries, including Japan, Australia, the United States and the United Kingdom. Each country has a special labelling scheme to show which food products have come from fair-trade farmers. This allows consumers to choose fair-trade products and contribute to a fairer and more sustainable system of food production.

By 2007, the fair-trade movement was working in 59 countries with around 600 producer

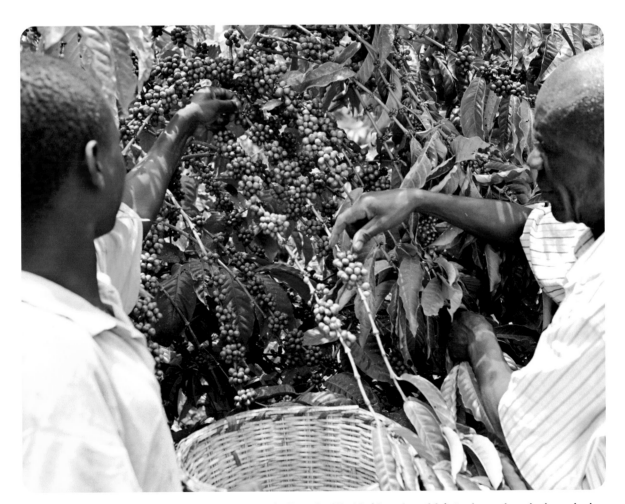

A farmer and his son pick fair-trade coffee beans in Uganda. Worldwide sales of fair-trade produce had reached £1.1 billion a year by 2007, with coffee one of the leading fair-trade products.

CASE STUDY

Ghana: Fair Cocoa

In Ghana, an elderly cocoa farmer carries a sack of beans from his farm to the co-operative's store, where he knows the scales will be accurate and he will be paid for the full weight of his crop. This story could be repeated time and again around the world, with farming co-operatives buying their own scales. It is one example of how earnings from fair-trade sales enable farmers to take more control over their businesses and their lives. The Kuapa Kokoo Co-operative in Ghana has 45,000 cocoa farmers and is one of the best-known success stories. As well as receiving fair prices for their beans, the Kuapa Kokoo farmers own one-third of the UK-based chocolate manufacturer Divine Chocolate Ltd. This means they also benefit from the value added to their beans when they are made into consumer products and sold.

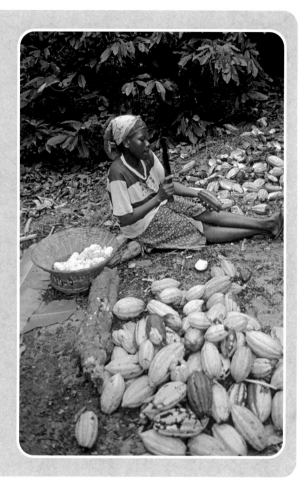

In Ghana, a woman works on a fair-trade cocoa plantation. Here, farmers are assured of a fair price for their produce.

organisations and over 650 traders. It was benefiting around seven million people – farmers, workers and their families – in LEDCs.

Success of the Movement

The growth of the fair-trade movement and its popularity with consumers has encouraged many major food companies to switch to fair-trade products. In the United States, 'Dunkin' Donuts' made all its espresso coffee fair trade in 2006, and the UK-based supermarket Sainsbury's opted to switch all its banana sales to fair trade during 2007. Despite these successes, fair trade still makes up a tiny proportion of global food trade and tends to focus on non-staple items such as chocolate, coffee, tea, honey, juices and fruit.

FACTS IN FOCUS
Fair Trade and Fairtrade

The term 'fair trade' refers to the idea of farmers earning a decent income from the growth and export of their goods. 'Fairtrade' refers more specifically to the labelling system controlled by Fairtrade Labelling Organisations International and the organisations that are part of it. The FLO is the body that sets the standards for fair trade and makes sure they are met.

Cattle-ranching is a valuable form of farming in countries like Brazil, but beef has one of the highest virtual-water costs of any food type.

Virtual Water

An important part of a sustainable future in food and water supplies is what experts call 'virtual water'. This is the amount of water that it takes to produce the food we eat – for example, in raising cattle, the amount of water it takes to irrigate pastures, to make the cattle feed and to process the meat. The amount of virtual water in meat is much more than in vegetables, so as increasing numbers of people around the world eat more meat, more water is used up.

When any type of food is traded around the world, so too is the water that was used to produce it. This has led to debate about where food should be grown in the future and whether it is sensible to always grow food locally, as many who promote sustainable food production suggest. If the country where the food is produced suffers from water shortages, it might be more sustainable to save the water used in producing food locally by importing food from a country with better water supplies instead.

Weighing it Up

Growing food or raising livestock in countries with sufficient water supplies could benefit countries where water is scarce – but only if

FACTS IN FOCUS
The Hidden Water in Our Food

Item	Litres of water per kilo
Wheat	1,200
Rice	2,700
Maize	450
Potatoes	160
Soya beans	2,300
Beef	15,000
Pork	6,000
Poultry	2,800
Eggs	4,700
Milk	900
Cheese	5,300

Source: UN Food and Agriculture Organisation

than is really needed. Trade only works if the end consumer is willing to buy, so consumer power can have a major impact on creating a more sustainable world. We all need food and water, and most of us enjoy access to both without too much trouble, but there remain millions who do not. The increasingly connected nature of our lives means that even the small changes we make can – through the power of trade – make a difference to development elsewhere.

What individuals choose to eat and where they go to buy their produce – a local market or a supermarket – may influence the food trade at a global level.

they can afford to buy the imported foods. With rising oil prices and increased food costs, buying in food (and the water it contains) could be too expensive for many countries, especially as those that suffer from a lack of water are also among the poorest in the world.

The idea of 'virtual water' has also been questioned by environmentalists, who are concerned about the negative impact of transporting even more food around the world. Weighing up the overall benefits of virtual water is still something scientists and major organisations such as the World Water Council are working on. One of their concerns is that it could make poorer countries too dependent on foreign trade. One way of addressing this issue might be to introduce a form of 'fair water trade', like the fair-trade movement in food supplies.

Consumer Power

Changing the way we think about food and water is perhaps one of the most effective ways to influence trade and distribution. Understanding where food comes from and how it is produced (including the water used) can help everyone to make informed choices. Only buying what we need to avoid waste, for example, would make sure that retailers and suppliers did not buy more

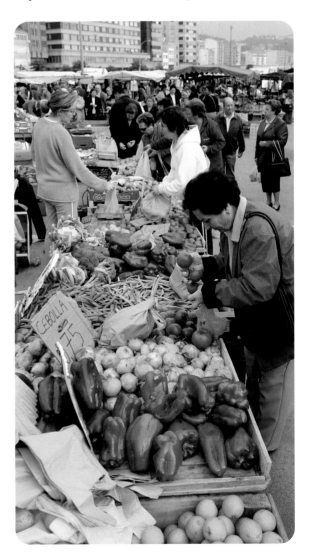

facts and figures

Population and Food Production (1965–2005)

Year	Population (thousands)	Crop yield (kg/ha)
1965	3,313,902	1,644
1970	3,675,901	1,838
1975	4,059,564	2,101
1980	4,431,033	2,319
1985	4,823,325	2,726
1990	5,263,923	2,900
1995	5,676,845	2,775
2000	6,076,654	3,073
2005	6,461,659	3,254

Source: World Development Indicators, 2008

Dietary Energy

Country/Region	kcal consumed/person/day
United States	3,770
United Kingdom	3,440
Russia	3,080
Brazil	3,060
South Africa	2,940
China	2,940
Japan	2,770
Peru	2,570
India	2,440
Thailand	2,410
Kenya	2,150
Democratic Republic of Congo	1,610
World average	*2,800*

Source: UN FAO, 2007

Coffee Prices

Year	Price (US cents per lb)
1980	213.07
1985	152.1
1990	70.36
1995	162.81
2000	97.68
2005	93.63
2008	127.93

Source: International Coffee Organisation, 2008

Food Miles

Food miles is the distance an item of food travels from the farm to the supermarket. This table shows a basket of 10 food items purchased in the UK and how many miles each item has travelled.

Item	Origin	Food miles
Apples	USA	10,133
Asparagus	Peru	6,312
Pears	Argentina	6,886
Spinach	Spain	958
Grapes	Chile	7,249
Potatoes	Israel	2,187
Tomatoes	Saudi Arabia	3,086
Chicken	Thailand	6,643
Brussels Sprouts	Australia	10,562
Carrots	South Africa	5,979

Further Resources

Websites

Friends of the Earth International
http://www.foei.org/

Greenpeace International
http://www.greenpeace.org/international/

Oxfam International
http://www.oxfam.org/

The UN Conference on Trade and Development
http://unctad.org/

UN Food and Agricultural Organisation
http://www.fao.org/

World Economic Forum
http://www.weforum.org/en/index.htm

World Trade Organisation
http://www.wto.org/

Books

Baines, John, *Food and Farming* (The Global Village), Evans Publishing, 2008

Baines, John, *Food for Life* (Sustainable Futures), Evans Publishing, 2005

Bowden, Rob, *Earth's Water Crisis* (What If We Do Nothing?), World Almanac, 2007

Bowden, Rob, *Sustainable World: Food and Farming*, Wayland, 2003

Bowden, Rob, *Trade* (The Global Village), Evans Publishing, 2008

Farndon, John, *From DNA to GM Wheat: Discovering Genetically Modified Food*, Heinemann Library, 2006

Inskipp, Carol, *Conserving Fresh Water* (Sustainable Futures), Evans Publishing, 2005

Kerr, Jim, *Food: Ethical Debates in What We Eat* (Dilemmas in Modern Science), Evans Publishing, 2007

Mason, Paul, *Food*, Raintree, 2004

Morgan, Sally, *Natural Resources* (The Global Village), Evans Publishing, 2008

Oxlade, Chris and Rufus Bellamy, *Food for All*, Franklin Watts, 2004

Wilkinson, Philip, *Food and Farming: Feeding an Expanding World*, Chrysalis, 2005

Glossary

agroforestry a method of farming in which trees and crops are grown together. The trees help keep nutrients in the soil and prevent soil erosion, so crops are improved.

arable land land that is suitable for growing crops.

biofuels fuels made from organic material. Biofuels are often made from plant sources, but they can also be created from animal waste. Biogas, bioethanol and biodiesel are examples of biofuels.

biotechnology the science of modifying plants and animals to have new characteristics for use in food and farming – for example, increasing a plant's immunity to disease.

calorie a unit used to measure how much energy something has. When used in relation to food, its full name is kilocalorie (Kcal).

certification a process in which an official body like a government or organisation ensures that an area or industry – such as organic farming – meets particular standards.

climate change a change in global temperatures that can result in extreme weather conditions. Climate change can happen naturally, but human activities are believed to be increasing the rate of this change.

deforestation the process of cutting down trees from an area so that the land can be used for purposes such as farming.

ecosystem a community of living plants, animals, insects, and the environment in which they live.

erosion the wearing away of soil or rocks by natural forces such as wind or water. Soil erosion can also be caused by human activity such as farming.

European Union an organisation of 27 European countries. The EU allows freedom of movement of people, goods, services and money between its member nations.

exports any goods or services that are sold outside the country in which they originate.

famine a period in which there is a severe shortage of food in a particular area.

fossil fuel a fuel made from living material over millions of years. Coal, oil and natural gas are examples of fossil fuels.

genetic modification the process of making some food products bigger, better or more resistant to disease by combining the genes of different species to develop the strongest characteristics.

greywater water that has been used for domestic purposes such as washing, which is then used for other purposes such as watering gardens.

groundwater water that has seeped below the surface of the Earth and often lies between the soil and rock. Groundwater supplies can be pumped to the surface and used for irrigation or drinking water.

human rights the basic rights and freedoms to which all people are considered entitled. These include rights such as freedom of expression, the right to legal protection and employment. They also include the right to enough food and water to be healthy.

hydroelectricity electricity generated from moving water.

imports any goods or services that originate outside the country in which they are purchased.

irrigation a system of watering dry land by digging ditches or otherwise diverting water sources to help crops grow.

LEDC less economically developed country – one of the poorer countries of the world. LEDCs include all of Africa, Asia (except Japan), Latin America and the Caribbean, and Melanesia, Micronesia and Polynesia.

MEDC more economically developed country – one of the richer countries of the world. MEDCs include the whole of Europe, North America, Australia, New Zealand and Japan.

processed food food that has been altered from its natural state, for example by freezing, drying or canning, or by the addition of preservatives or colourings.

resource a useful or valuable substance. Food and water are both resources.

rural relating to the countryside.

staple crops such as wheat or maize that provide the basic foodstuff for millions of people.

subsidy a grant of money that is made by a government to either a domestic seller or a buyer to help cover the cost of producing or selling certain goods and services.

surplus a quantity of a product such as a food crop that is larger than needed.

sustainability the use of resources in a way that means the present generation can have what it needs without damaging the supply of resources for future generations.

tariff a tax placed on goods transported from one country to another, or when they are imported. A tariff raises the price of imported goods, making them less competitive with goods that have been produced locally.

United Nations an international organisation, established in 1945, which aims to help countries cooperate in matters of international law, economic and social development, and human rights. There are currently 192 member states in the United Nations.

urban relating to built-up areas such as towns and cities.

urbanisation the process in which increasing numbers of people are settling in towns and cities. As urbanisation takes place, towns and cities grow larger and expand on to previously undeveloped land.

yield the amount of crops that a farmer can produce.

Index